Ichabod's *Adventure*

in Alphabet Town

by *Janet McDonnell*
illustrated by *Pam Peltier*

created by Wing Park Publishers

CHILDRENS PRESS®
CHICAGO

Library of Congress Cataloging-in-Publication Data

McDonnell, Janet, 1962-
    Ichabod's adventure in Alphabet Town / by Janet McDonnell ;
illustrated by Pam Peltier.
      p.   cm. — (Read around Alphabet Town)
    Summary: Ichabod the iceman meets "i" words on his
adventure in Alphabet Town. Includes activities.
    ISBN 0-516-05409-0
    [1. Alphabet—Fiction.]   I. Peltier, Pam, ill.   II. Title.
III. Series.
PZ7.M478436Id   1992
[E]—dc 20   91-20547
                                        CIP
                                        AC

Ichabod's *Adventure*

in Alphabet Town

You are now entering Alphabet Town,
With houses from "A" to "Z."
I'm going on an "I" adventure today,
So come along with me.

This is the "I" house of Alphabet Town. An iceman lives here.

His name is Ichabod, and he sells ice. Ichabod likes "i" things. Most of all, he likes selling ice.

But one day, Ichabod ran out
of ice.

"I will go to the icy sea and chop
more," he said.

He put on his

ice skates.

Then he took his ice ax, and off he went.

Ichabod skated far north. He skated past some

igloos,

all the way to the icy sea.

Then Ichabod took off his ice skates.
He walked out onto the ice.

As he chopped ice, he sang, "The iceman's life is the life for me. I skate all the way to the icy sea."

He chopped and chopped. But then,
Ichabod made a mistake. Guess what
happened?

He chopped off a big piece of ice.
It began to drift away with
Ichabod.

"Oh, no," said Ichabod. "I am on an

iceberg.

What will I do?"

"I must think," said Ichabod.
As he floated along, the day grew
hotter. Guess what happened next?

"My iceberg is melting!" cried Ichabod. And it was. Inch by inch, it was getting smaller. Ichabod was so afraid. "What will I do? What will I do?" he cried.

Just then, Ichabod saw an island.

"Yippie!" said Ichabod.

He jumped off the little iceberg
and swam to the island.

Now he was safe. But the island sand was hot and itchy. "Ick," said Ichabod.

By now, Ichabod was hungry. "I sure would like some

ice cream,"

he said.

He looked about. He saw lots of

ivy.

And he saw lots of

iguanas.

But no ice cream.

Just then an island boy came by.
"Hi," he said. "You are welcome here."

And he took Ichabod around the tiny
island.

He could see that Ichabod was hungry.
So he invited him to an

inn

for lunch. Guess what Ichabod had
for dessert? Ice cream!

"Do you like our island?" asked
the boy.

"I do," said Ichabod. "But I must find
a way to get back to Alphabet Town."

"I have an idea," said the island
boy. And off he went.

Soon he came back with a rubber boat.

Ichabod inflated it with air. He thanked the island boy and said good-bye.

Then off he sailed, singing,

"The iceman's life is the life for me.
I'm sailing home far across the sea."

MORE FUN WITH ICHABOD

What's in a Name?

In my "i" adventure, you read many "i" words. My name begins with an "I." Many of my friends' names begin with "I" too. Here are a few.

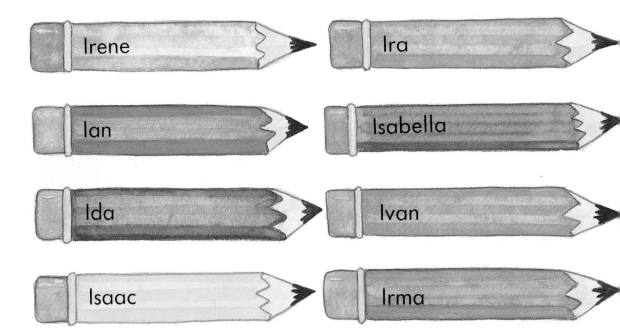

Irene

Ira

Ian

Isabella

Ida

Ivan

Isaac

Irma

Do you know other names that start with "I"?
Does your name start with "I"?

Ichabod's Word Hunt

I like to hunt for words with "i" in them. Can you help me find the words on this page that begin with "i"? How many are there? Can you read the words?

ship

Indian

taxi

insect

ball

kite

ski

Can you find any words with "i" in the middle?
Can you find any with "i" at the end?
Can you find a word with no "i"?

Ichabod's Favorite Things

"I" is my favorite letter. Can you guess why? I love "i" things. You can find some of my favorite "i" things in my house on page 7. How many "i" things can you find there? Can you think of more "i" things?

Now you make up an "i" adventure.